TABLE OF CONTENTS

Armadillo

Armadillos are known
for their hard outer shell.

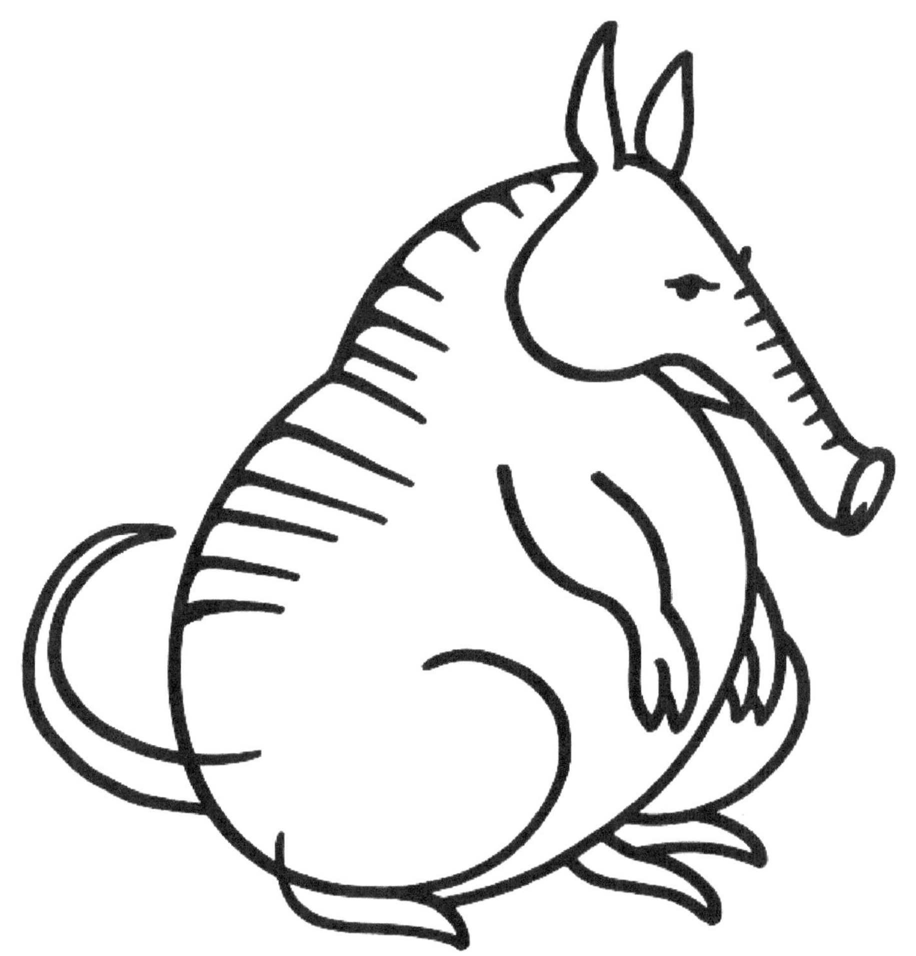

Buffalo

Buffalos are large members
of the Bovidae family.

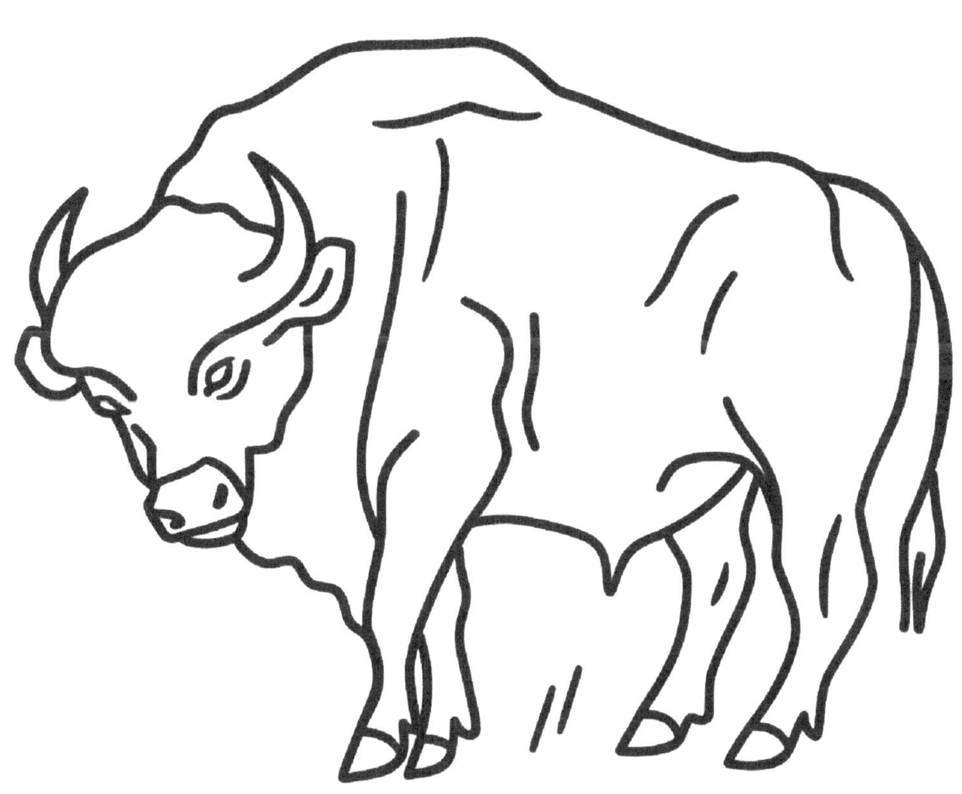

Cheetah

Cheetahs are the fastest land animals, reaching speeds up to 75 mph.

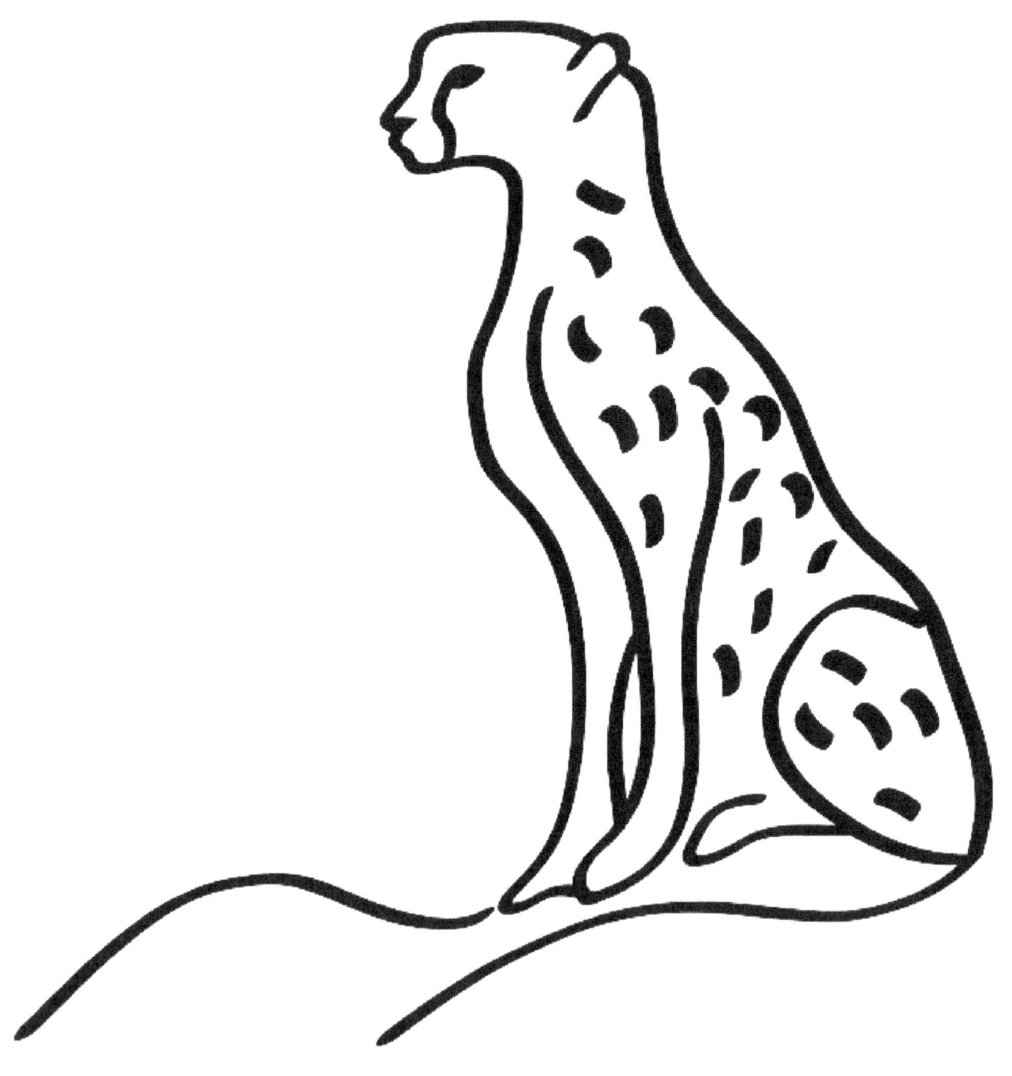

Dolphin

Dolphins are highly intelligent marine mammals known for their playful behavior.

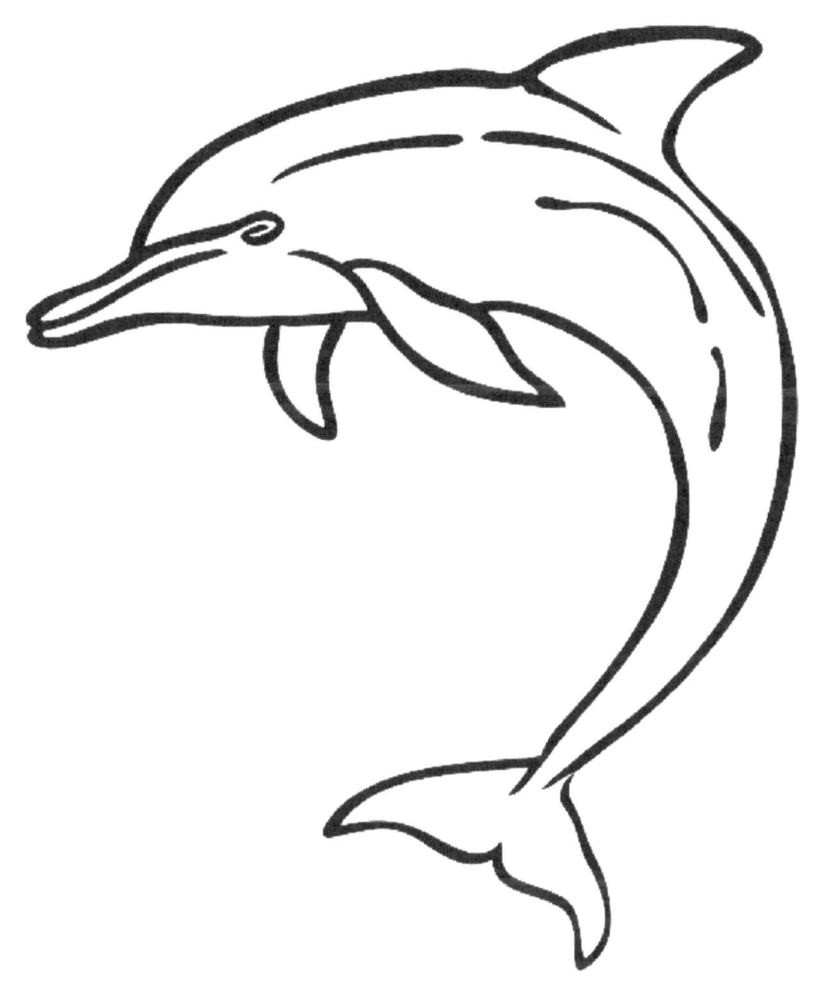

Elephant

Elephants are the largest land animals, with complex social structures.

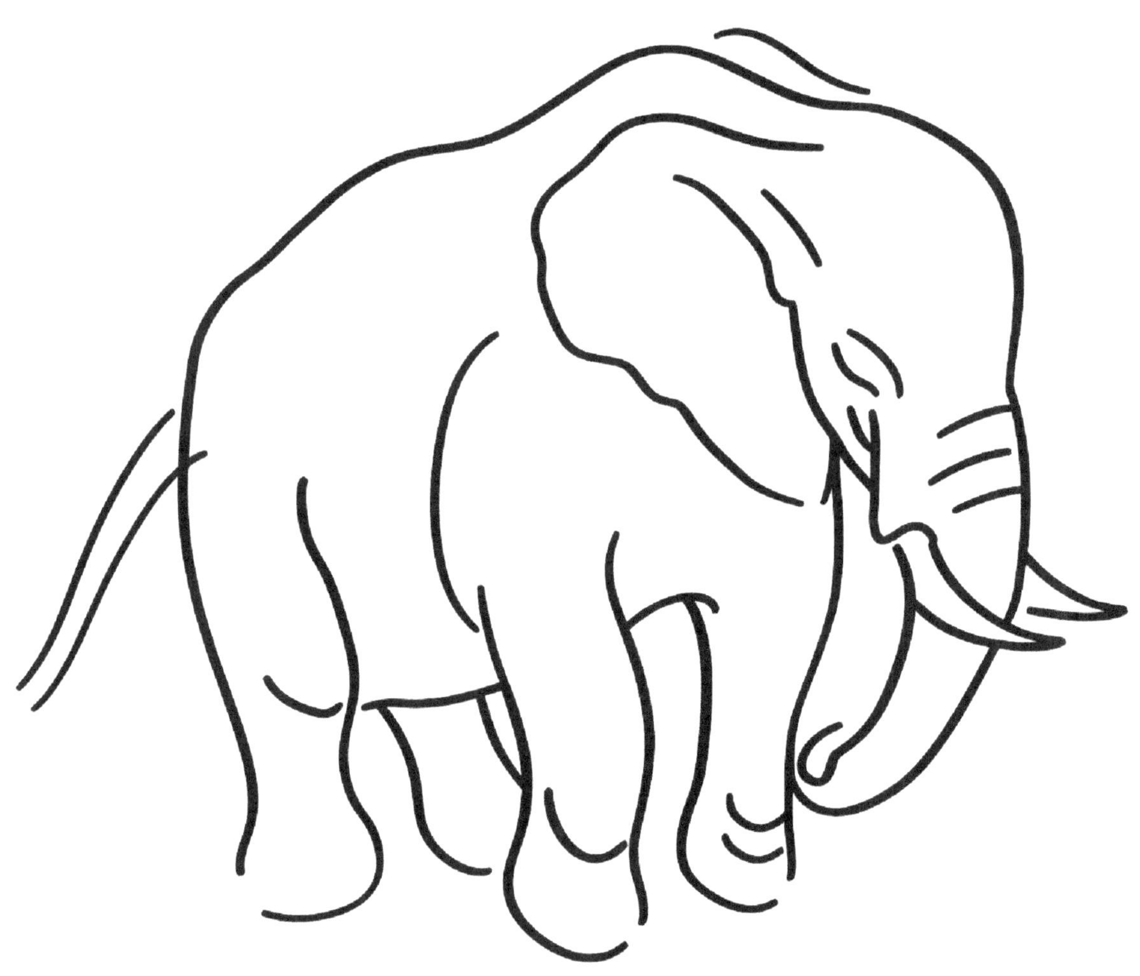

Flamingo

Flamingos are famous for their pink feathers, which come from their diet.

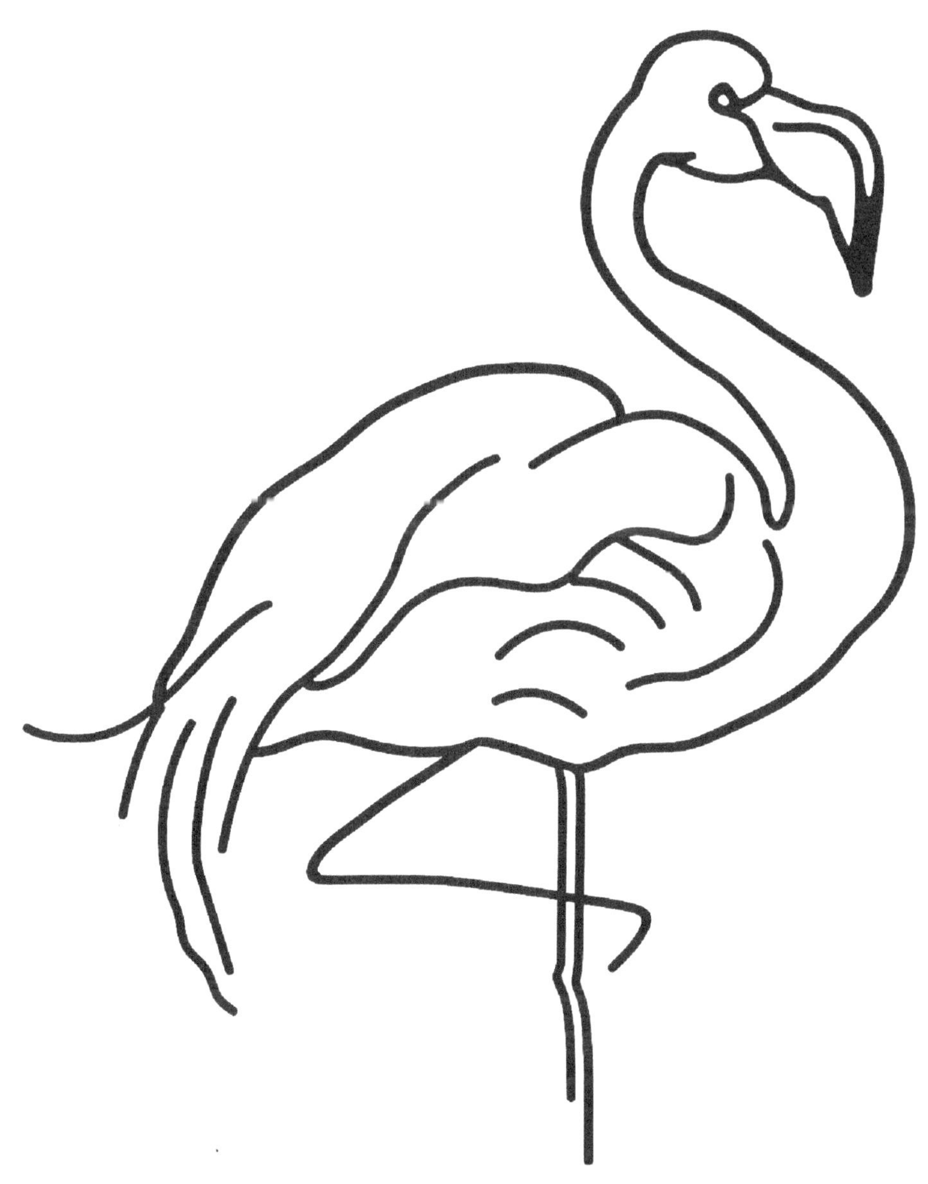

Giraffe

Giraffes are the tallest mammals
on Earth, with long necks and legs.

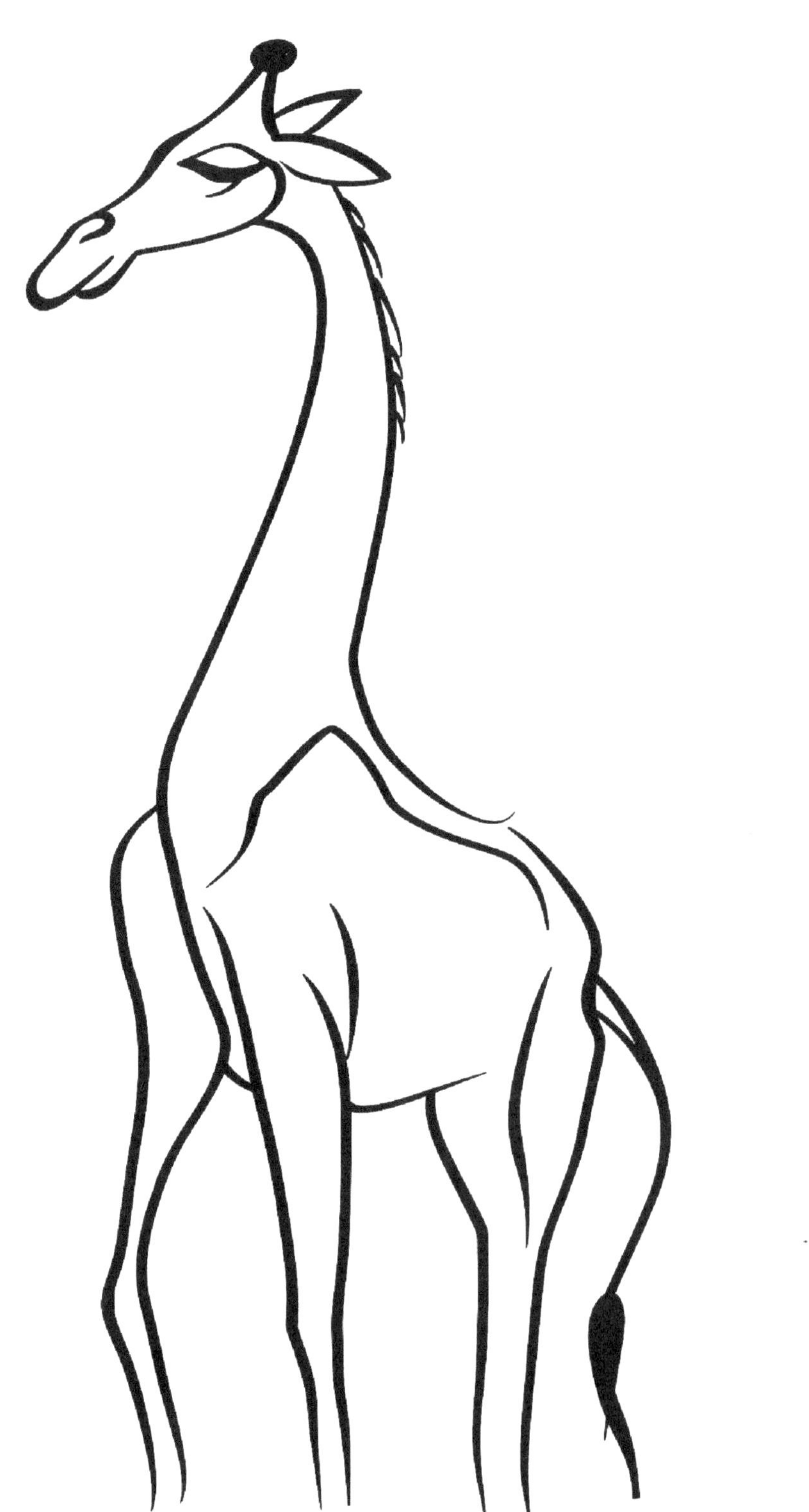

Hippopotamus

Hippopotamuses spend most of their day submerged in water to stay cool.

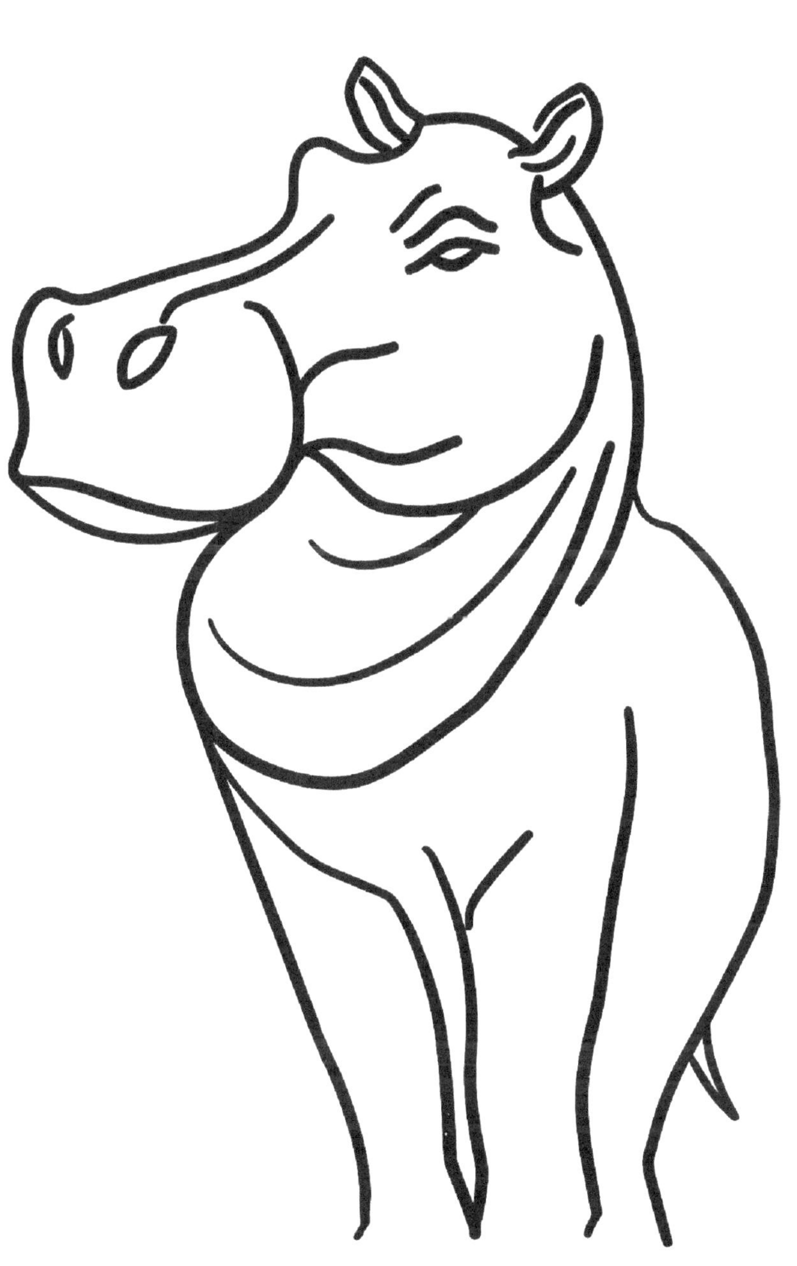

Iguana

Iguanas can change color based
on their mood and environment.

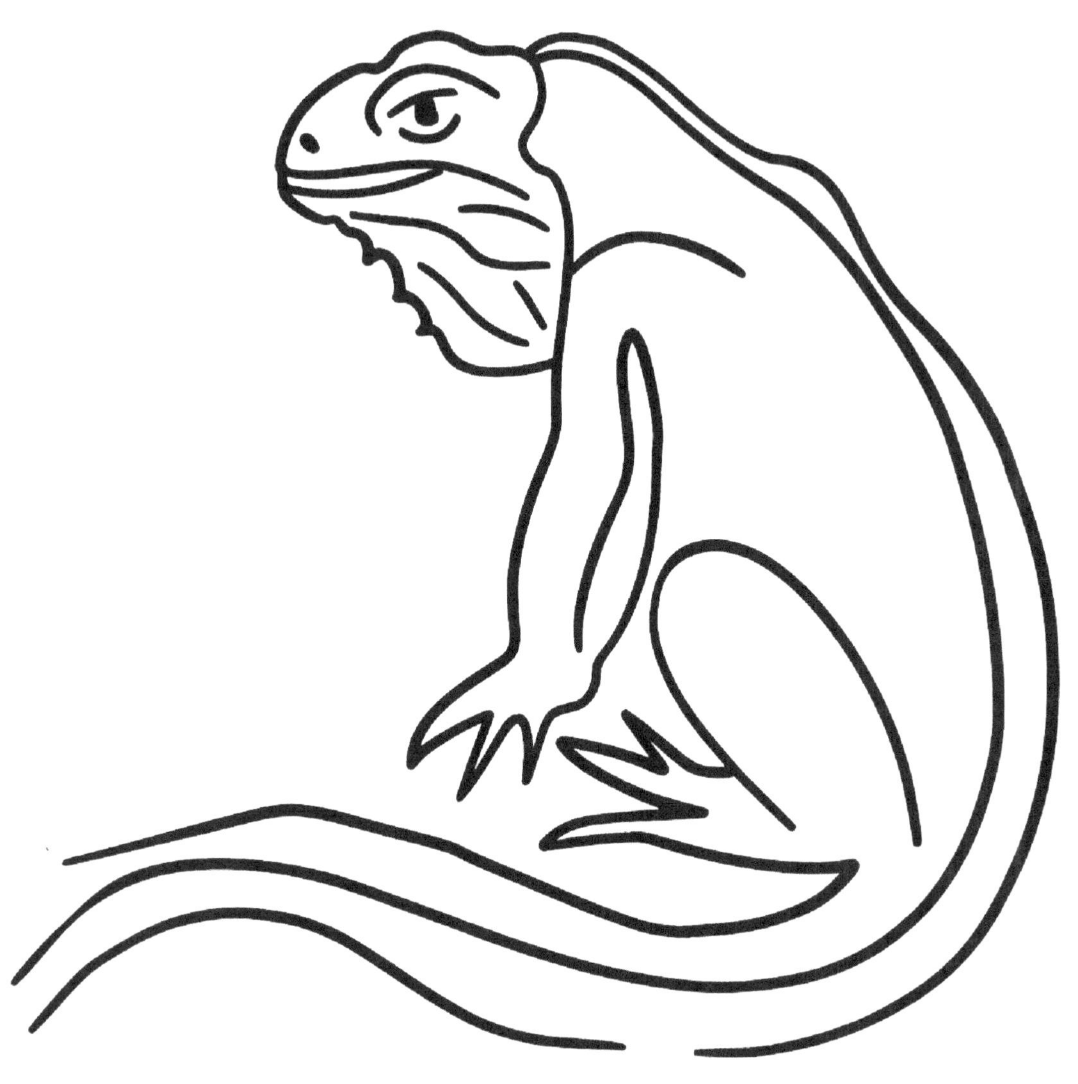

Jaguar

Jaguars are powerful predators with a bite strong enough to pierce turtle shells.

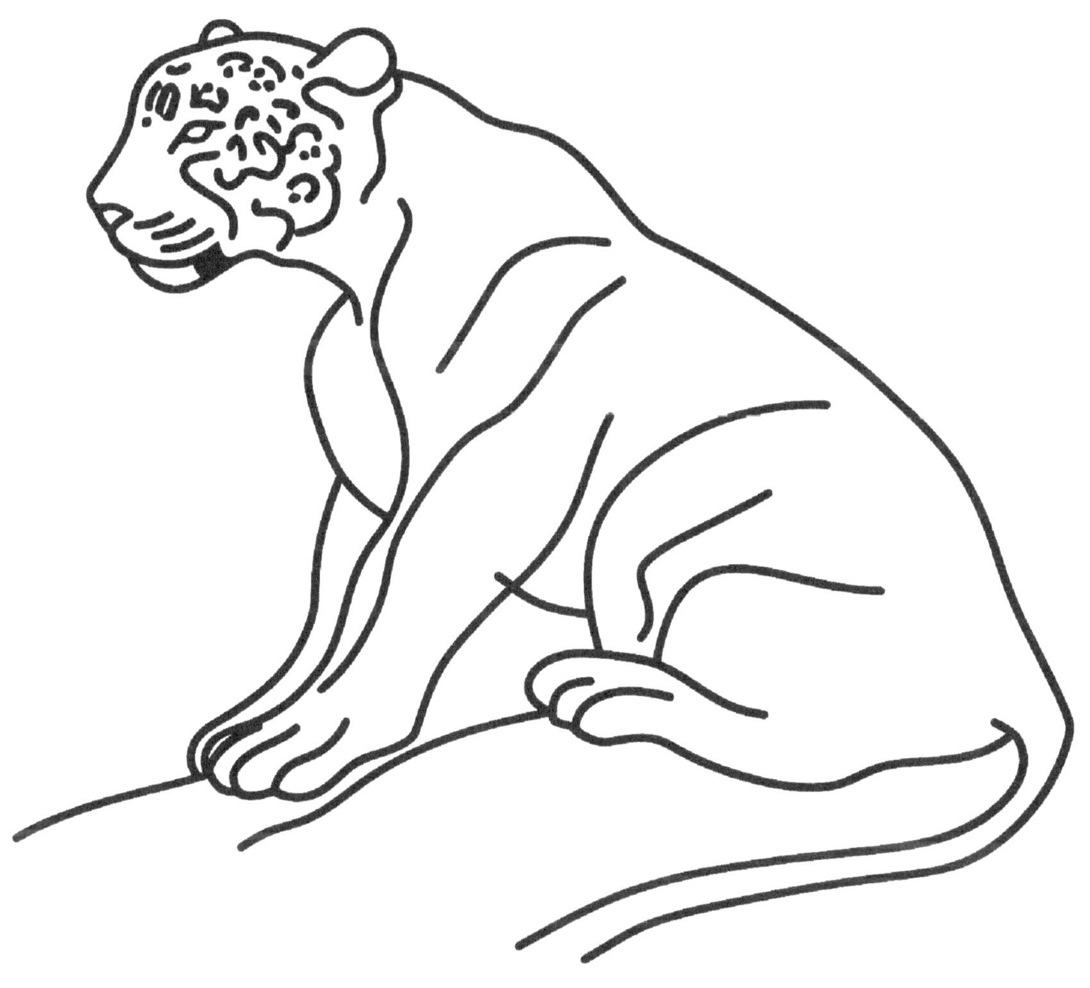

Koala

Koalas are marsupials that spend most
of their time sleeping in eucalyptus trees.

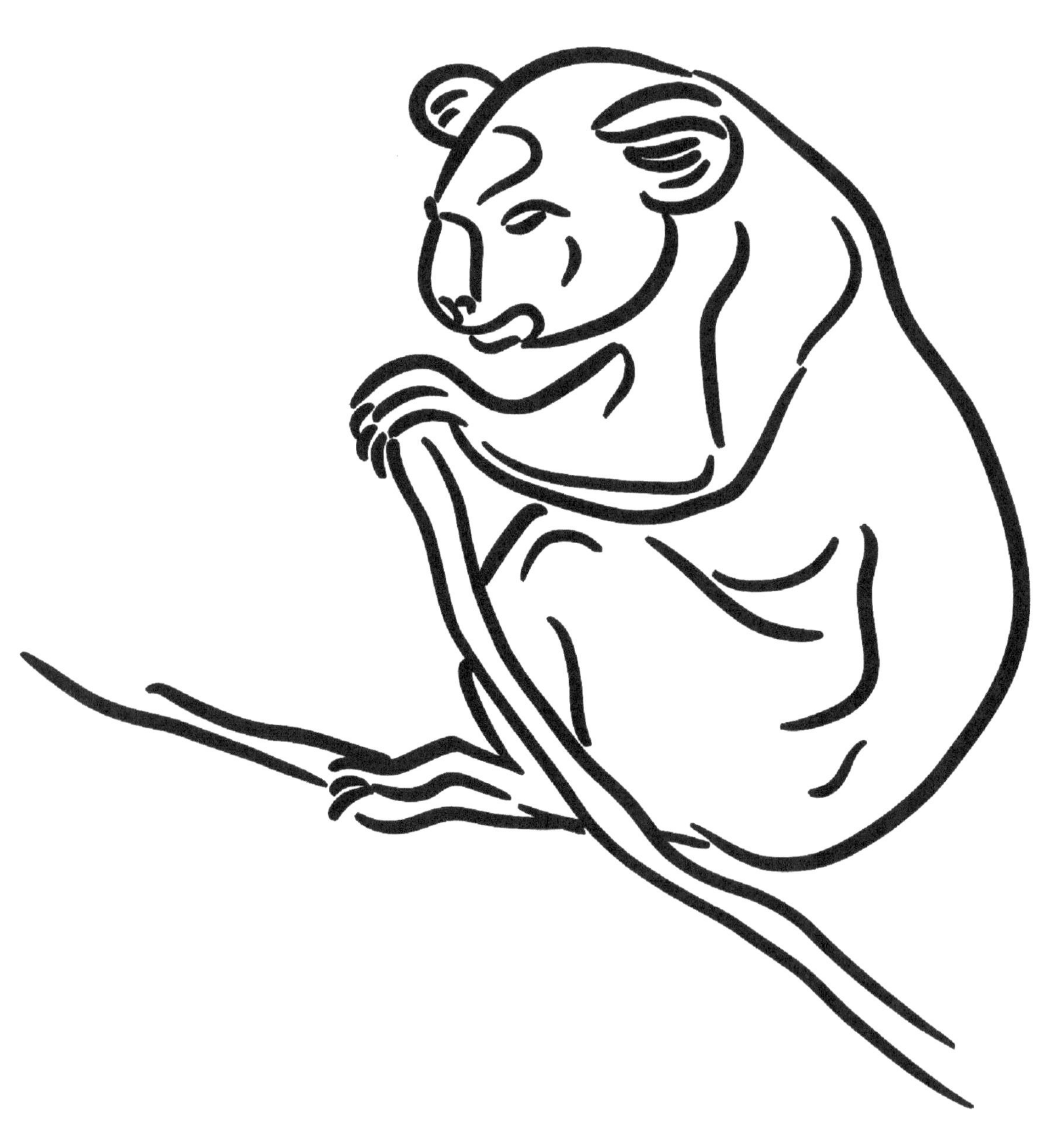

Lemur

Lemurs are unique to Madagascar and are known for their long, bushy tails.

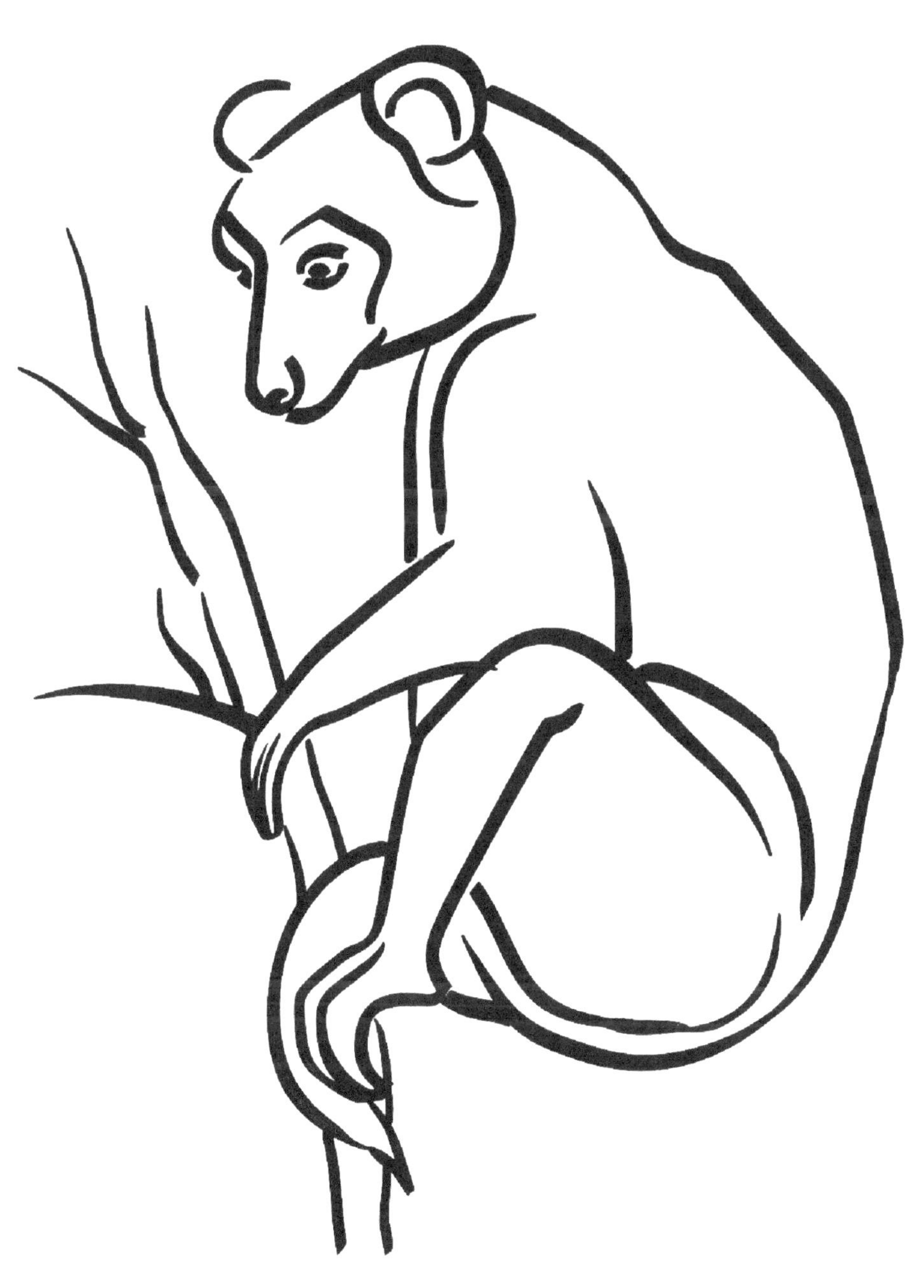

Meerkat

Meerkats are social animals that
live in groups called mobs or gangs.

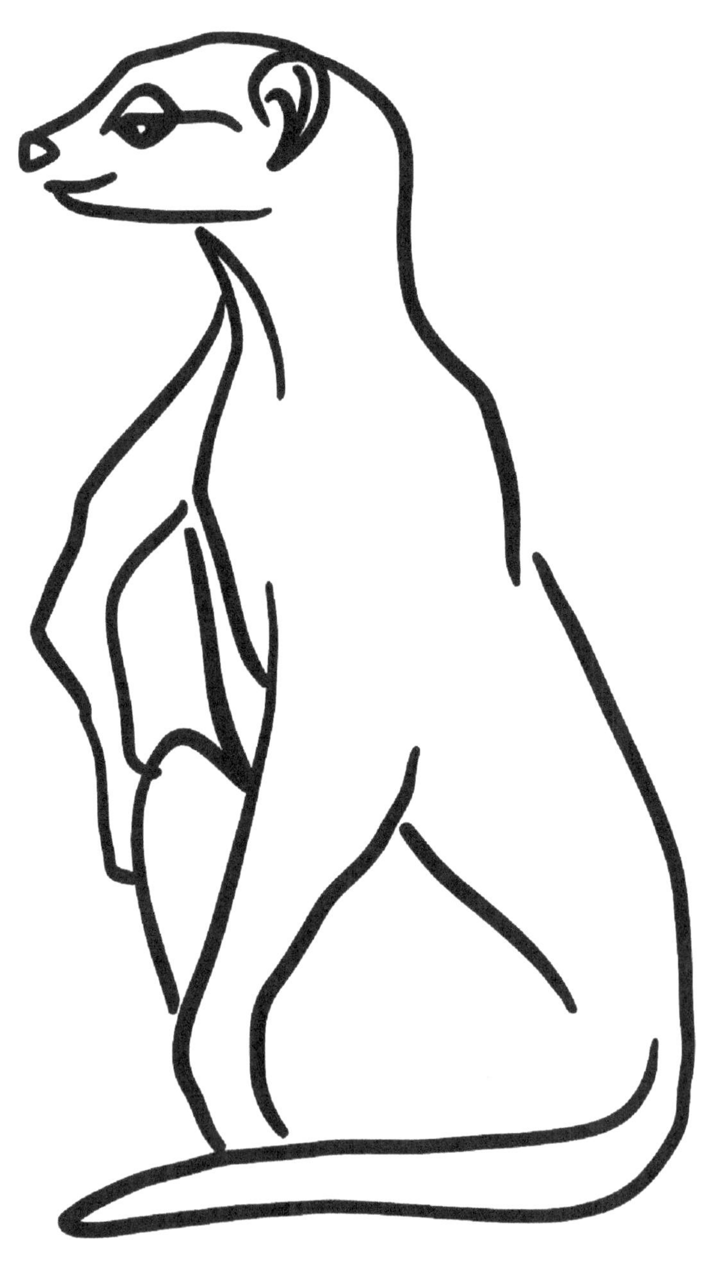

Narwhal

Narwhals are known as the 'unicorns of the sea' for their long, spiraled tusks.

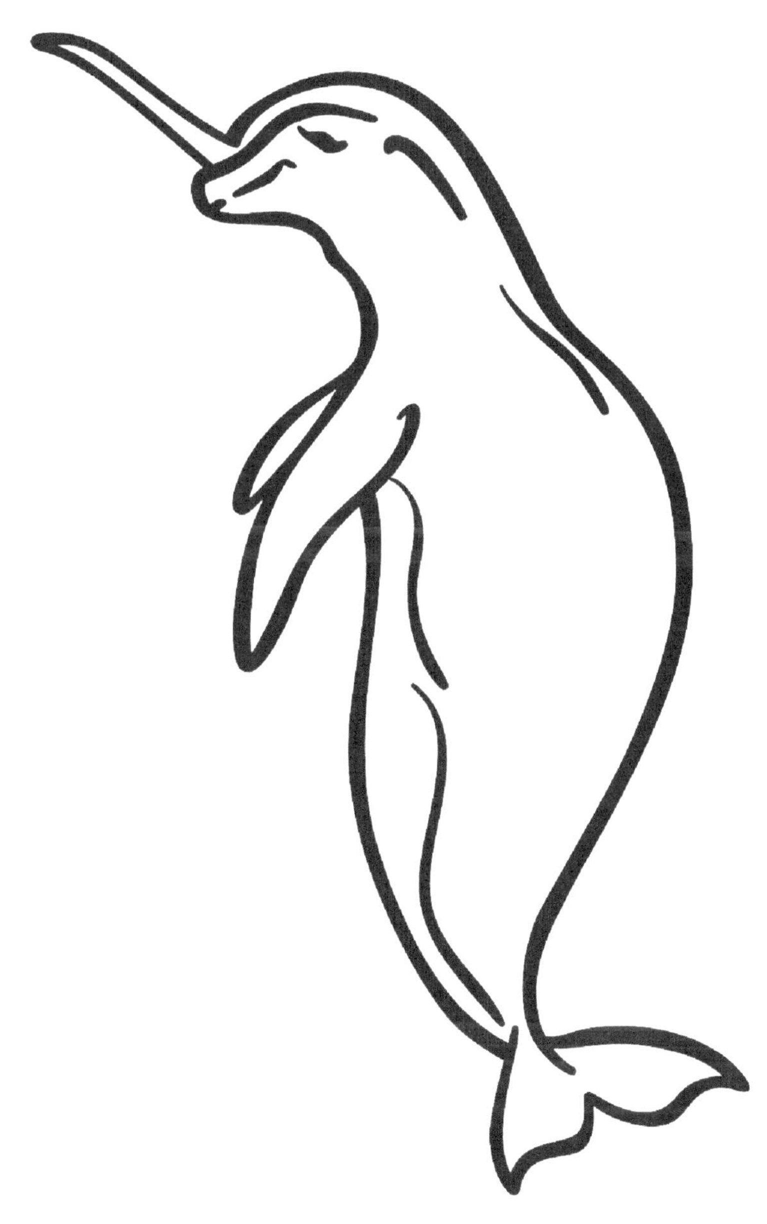

Octopus

Octopuses have three hearts
and can change color to blend
into their surroundings.

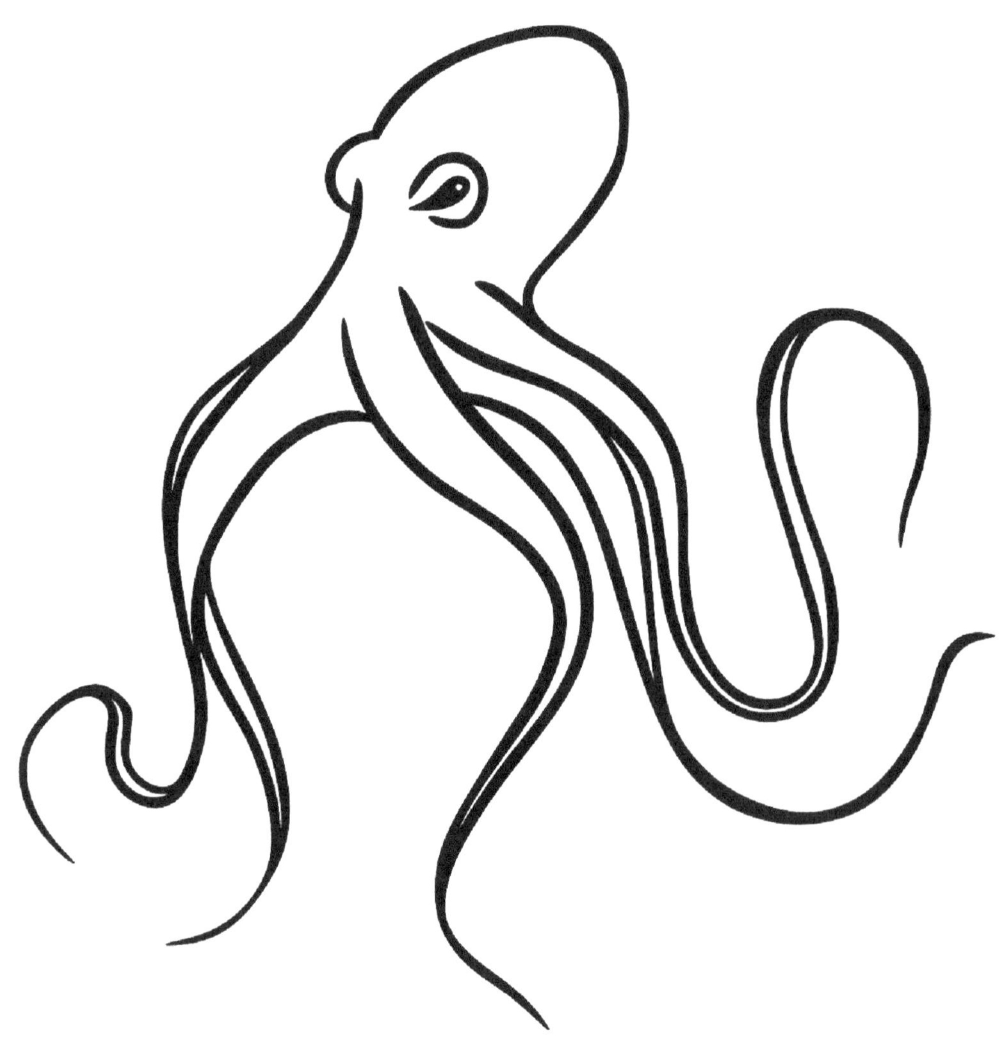

Penguin

Penguins are flightless birds
that are excellent swimmers.

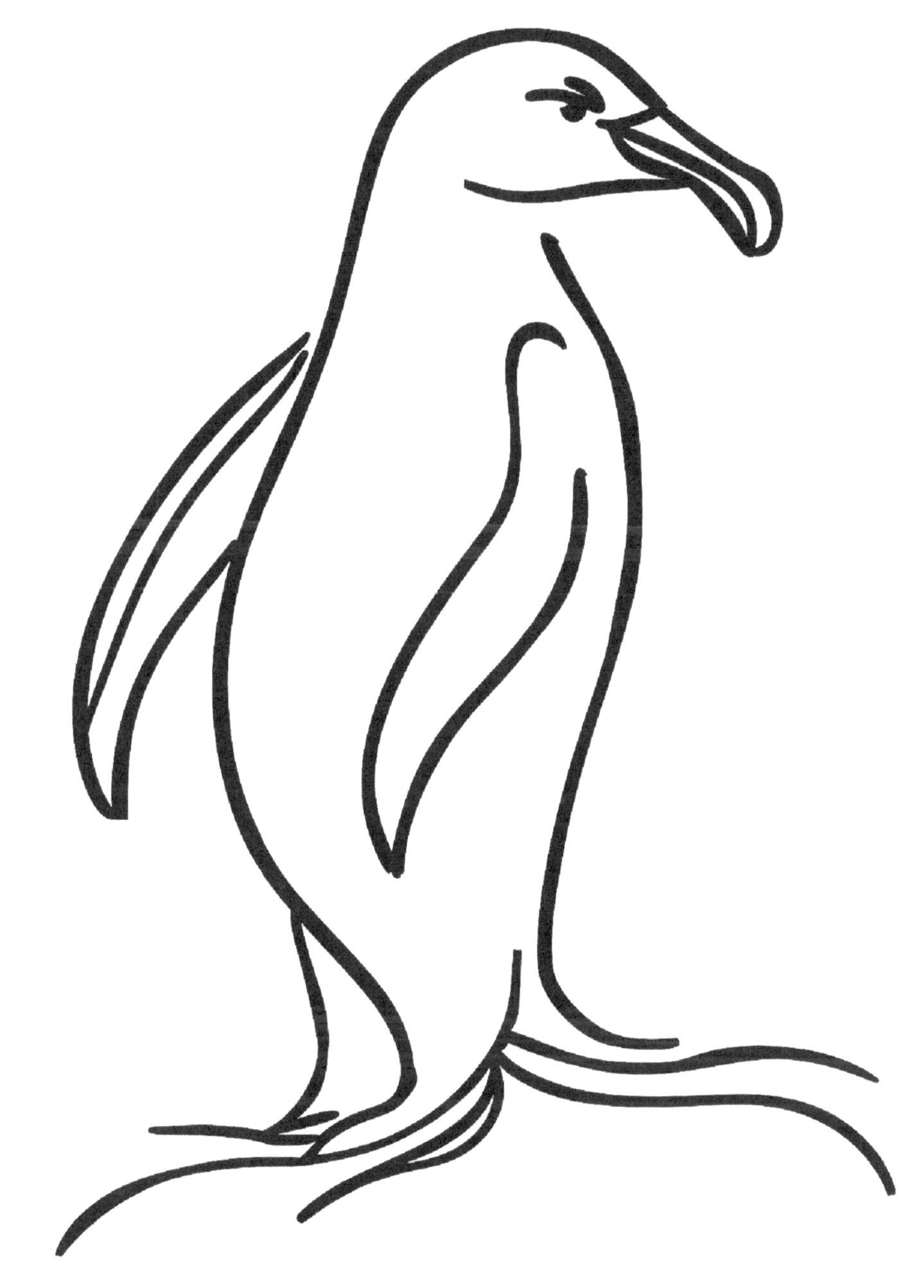

Quail

Quails are small, plump terrestrial birds known for their distinctive call.

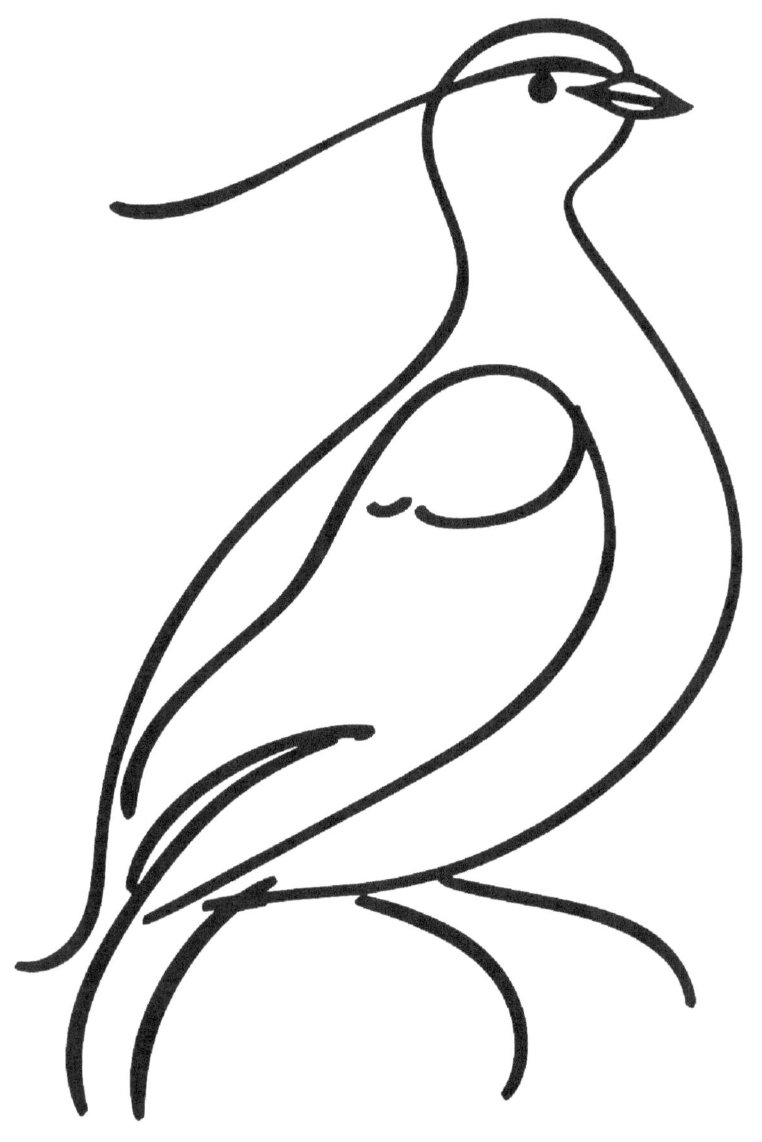

Rhino

Rhinos are characterized by their large size and protective skin.

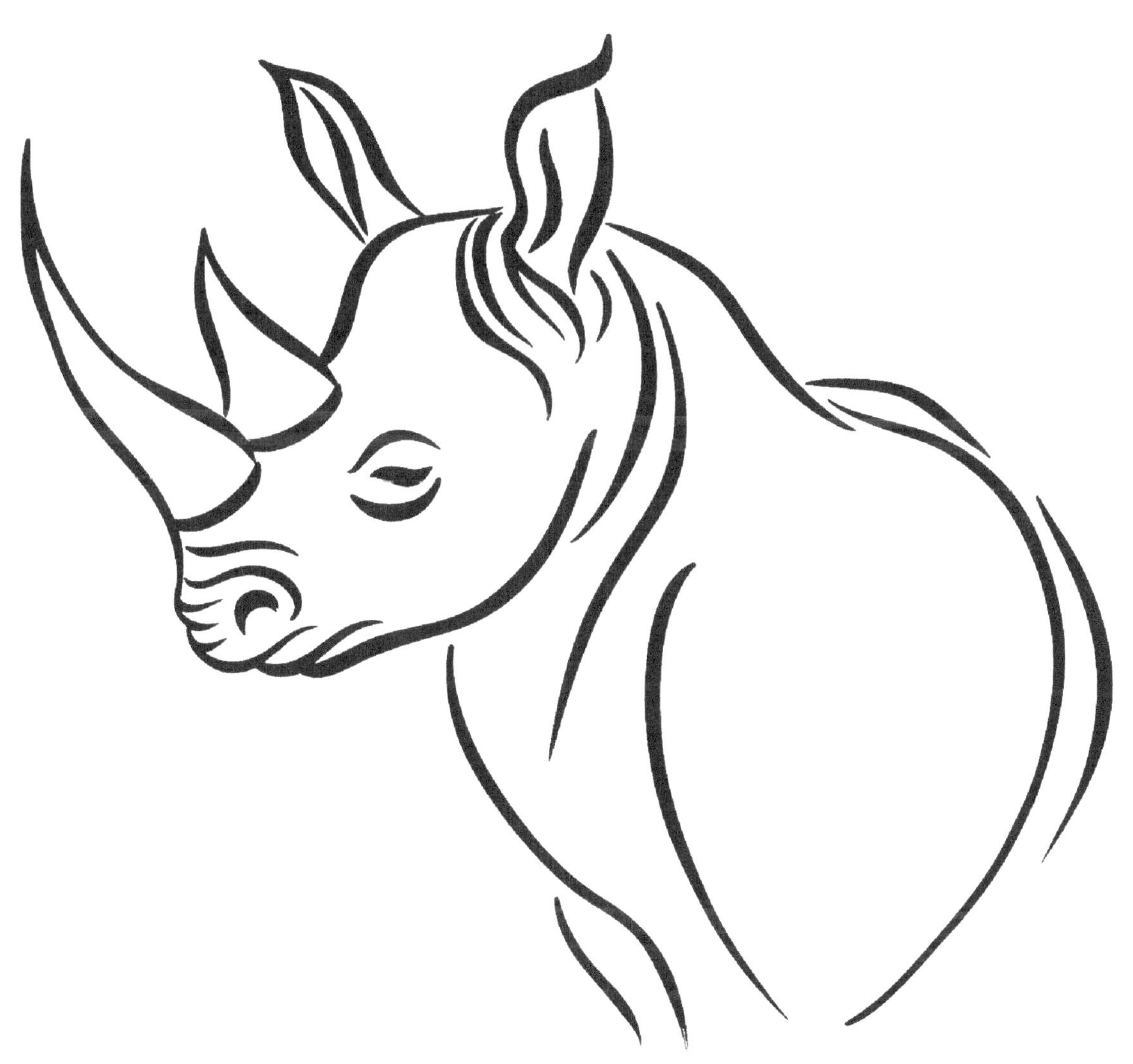

Sloth

Sloths are known for their slow movement and spending most of their life hanging upside down.

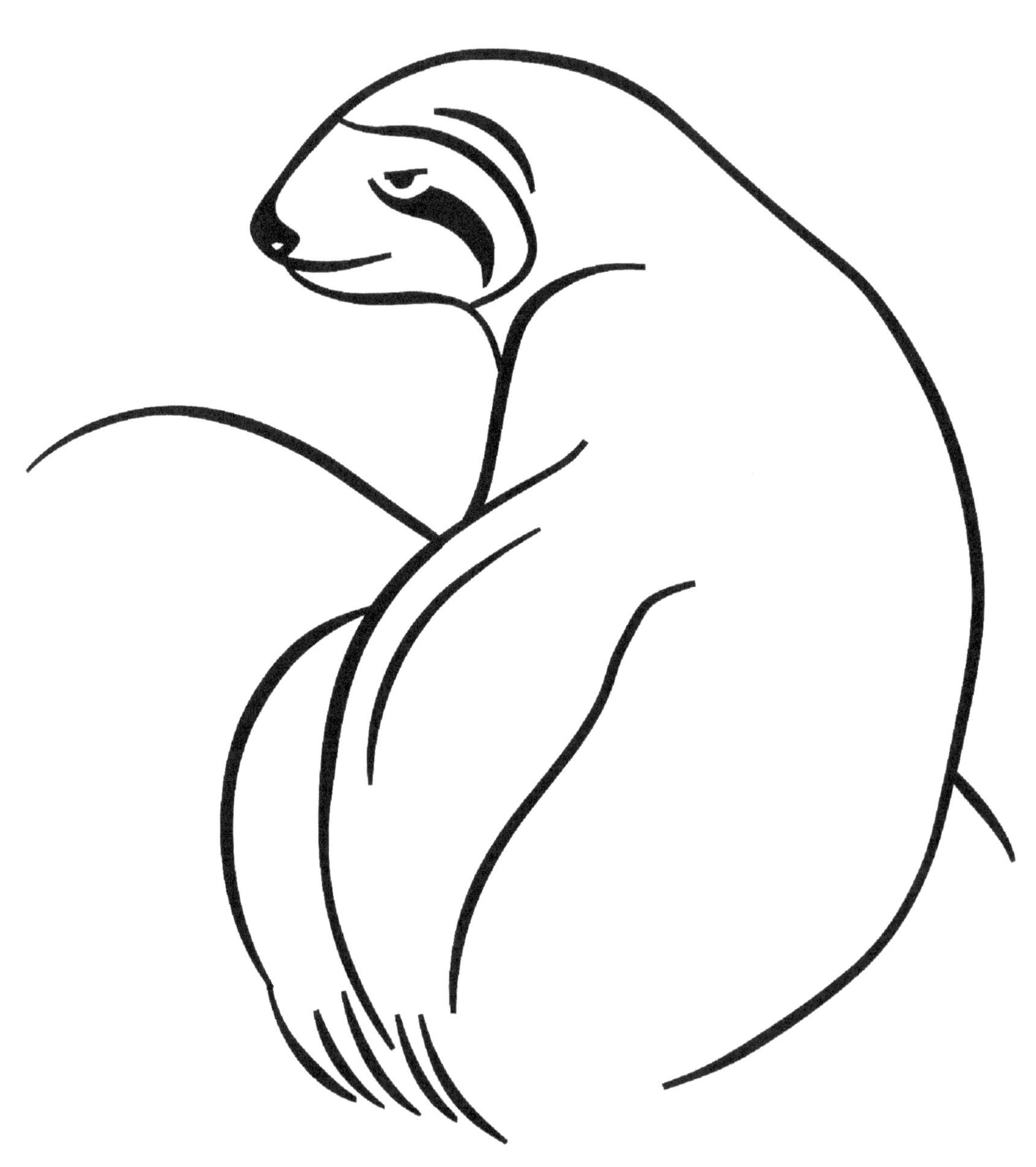

Tiger

Tigers are the largest cat species, recognizable by their dark vertical stripes.

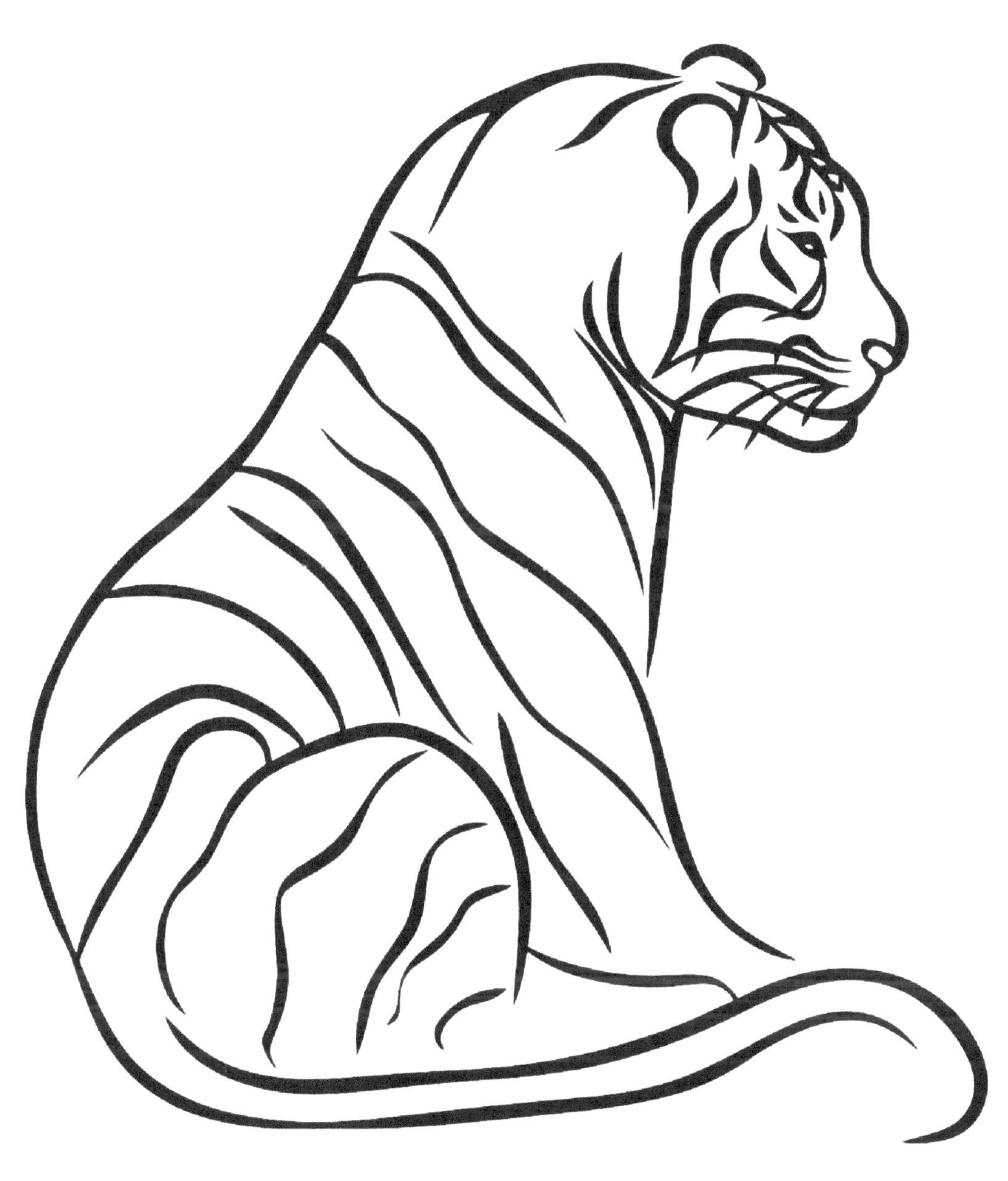

Urchin

Urchins are small, spiny sea creatures, often found in oceans around the world.

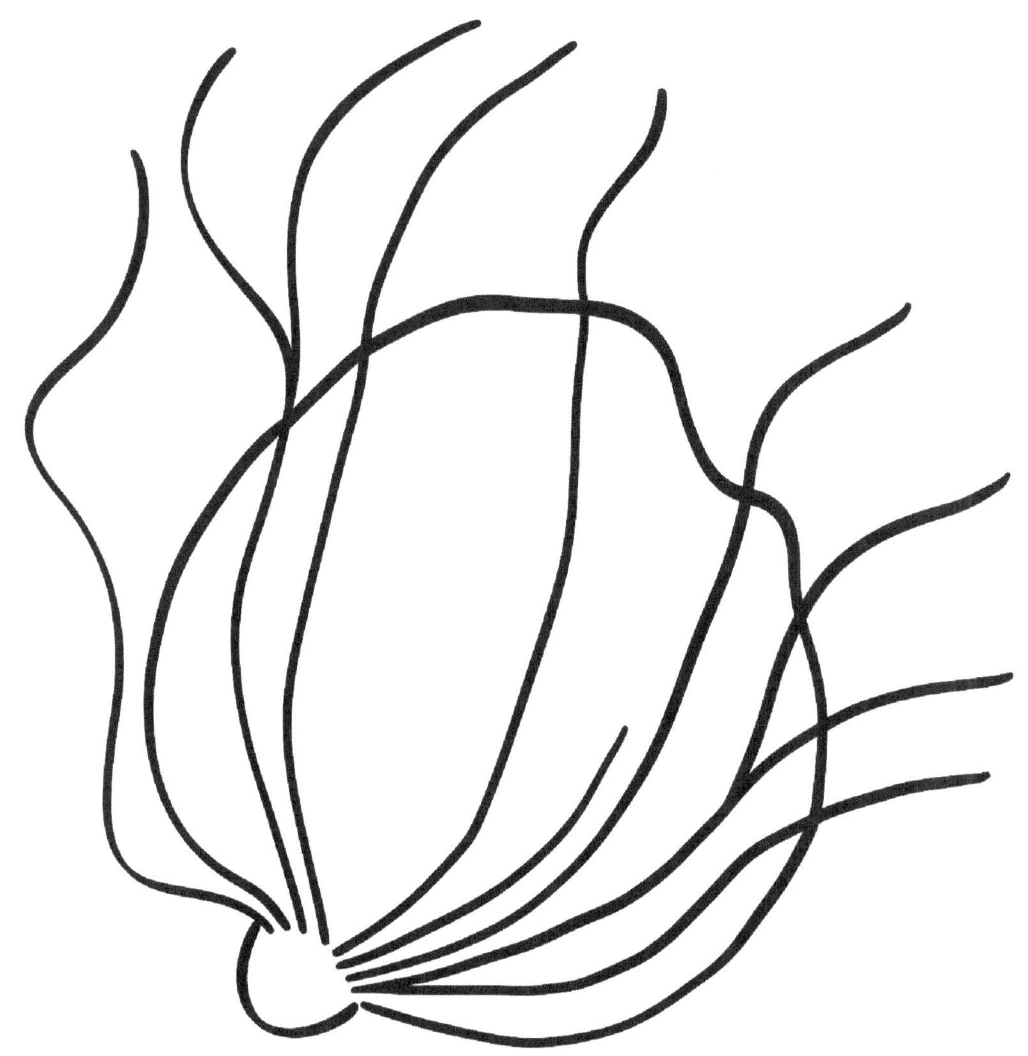

Vulture

Vultures play an important role in the ecosystem by scavenging dead animals.

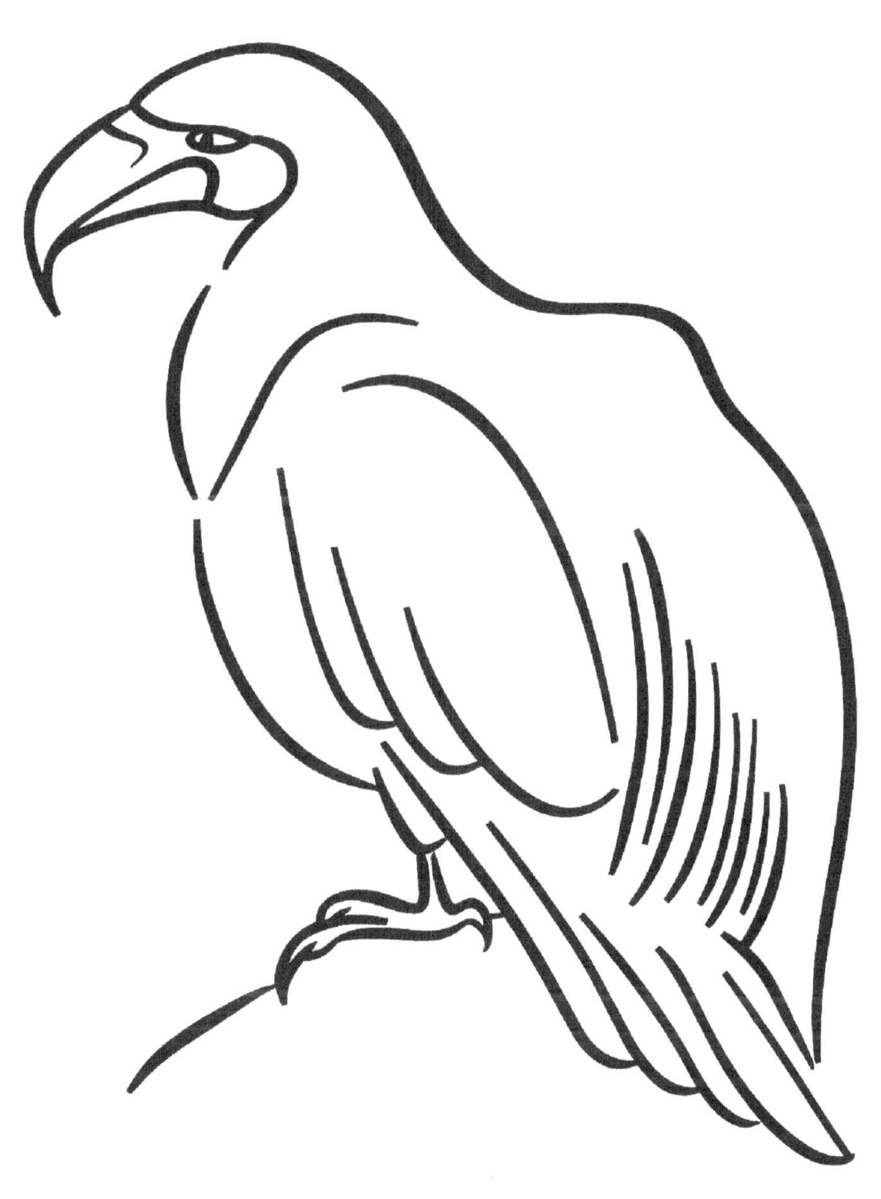

Walrus

Walruses are known for their
distinctive tusks and large size.

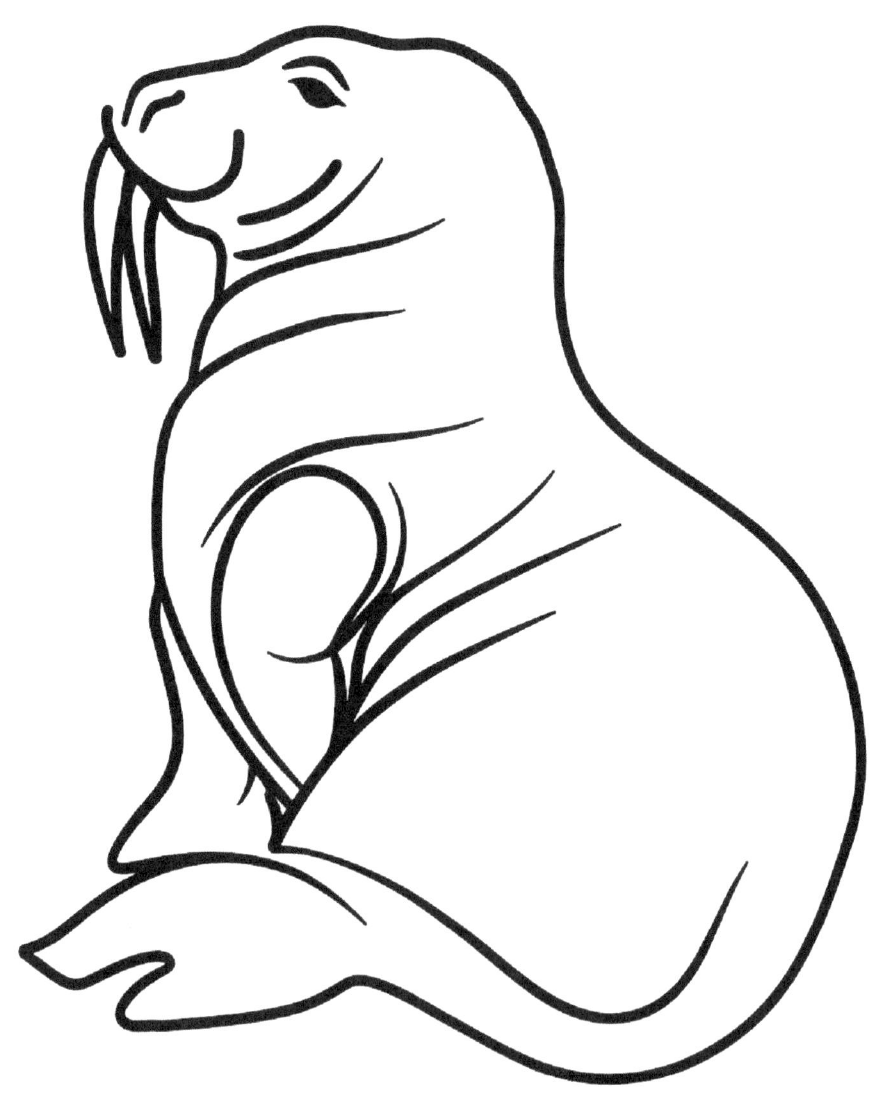

X-ray fish

X-ray fish are small, translucent fish,
allowing their skeleton to be seen.

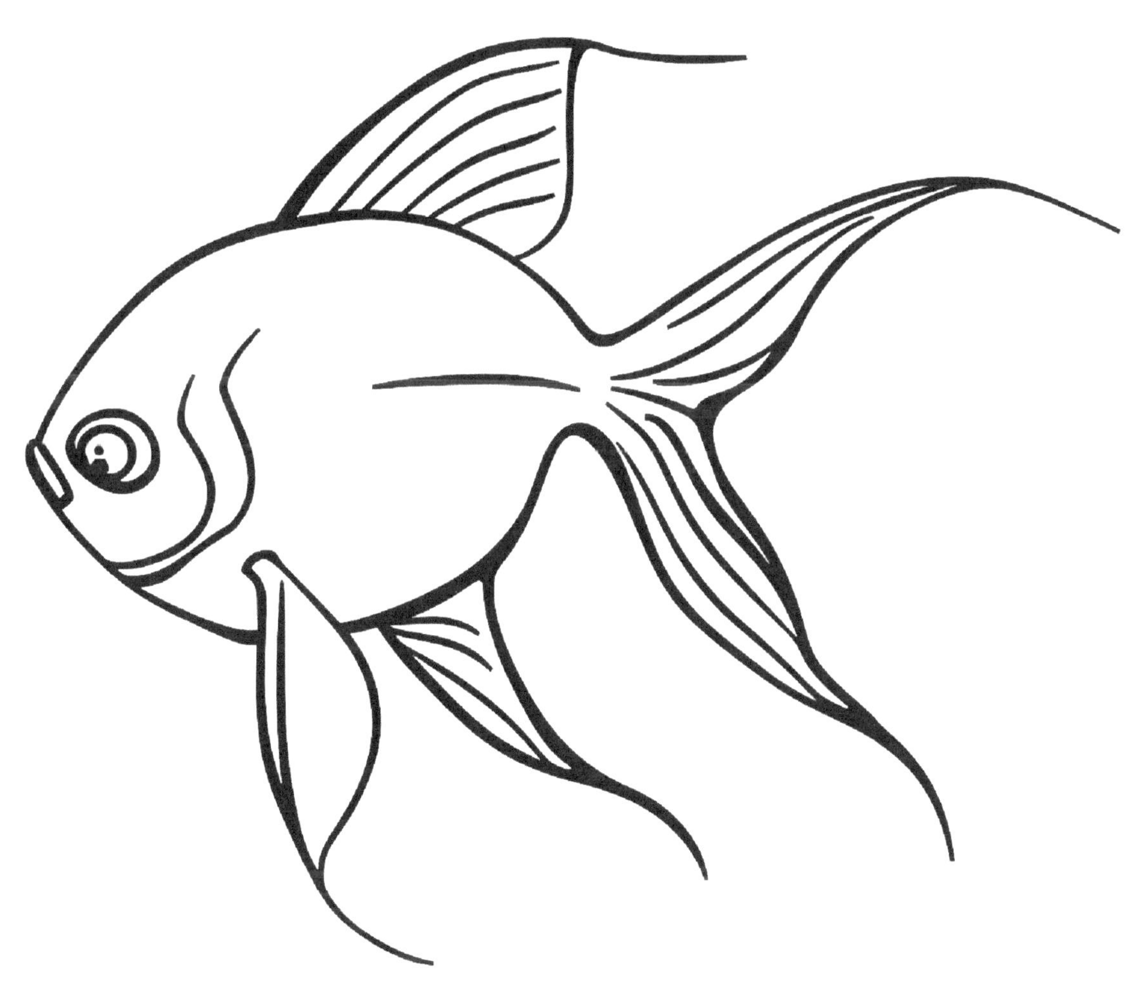

Yak

Yaks are adapted to high altitudes,
with thick fur to keep them warm.

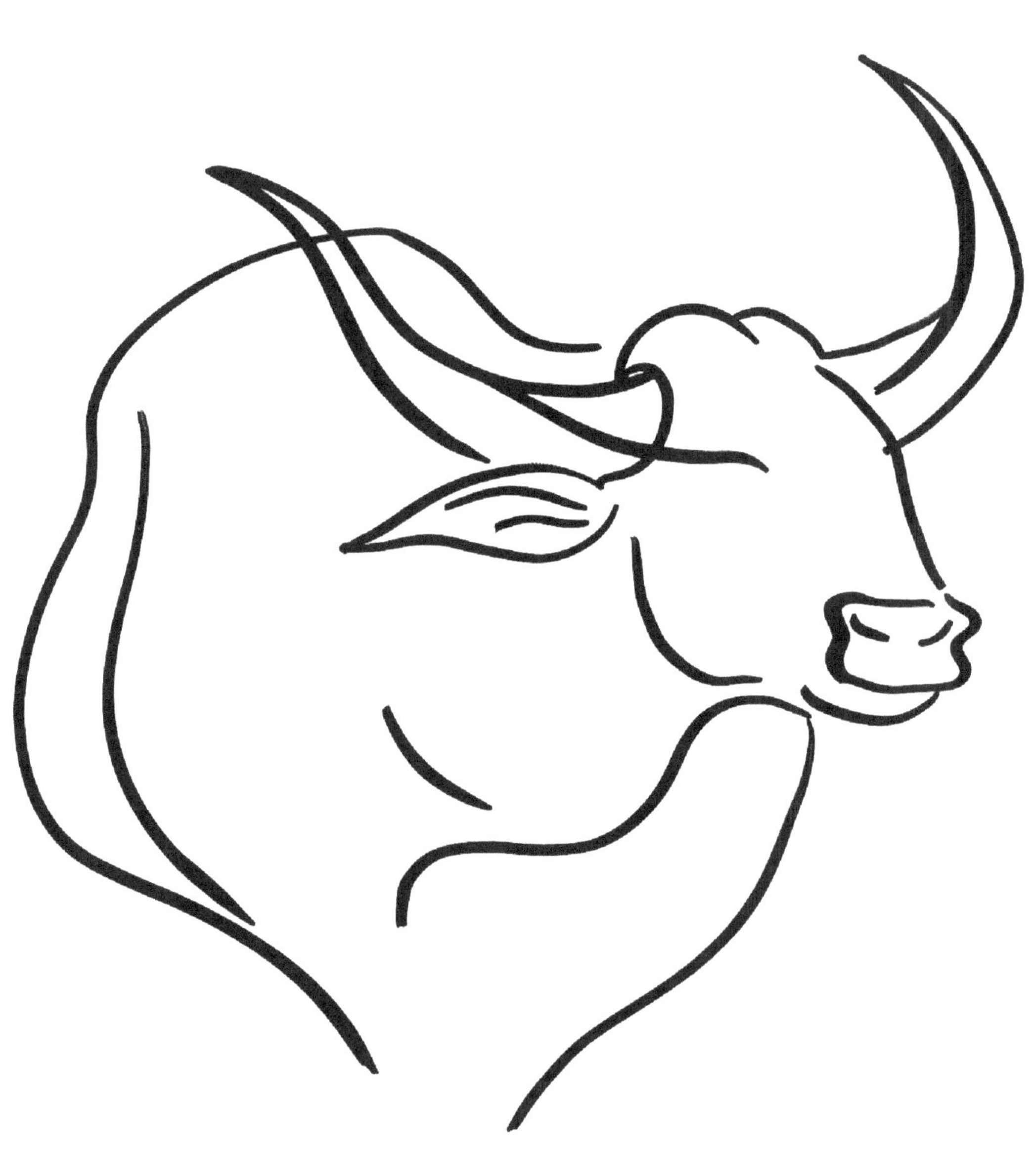

Zebra

Zebras are known for their
distinctive black and white stripes.

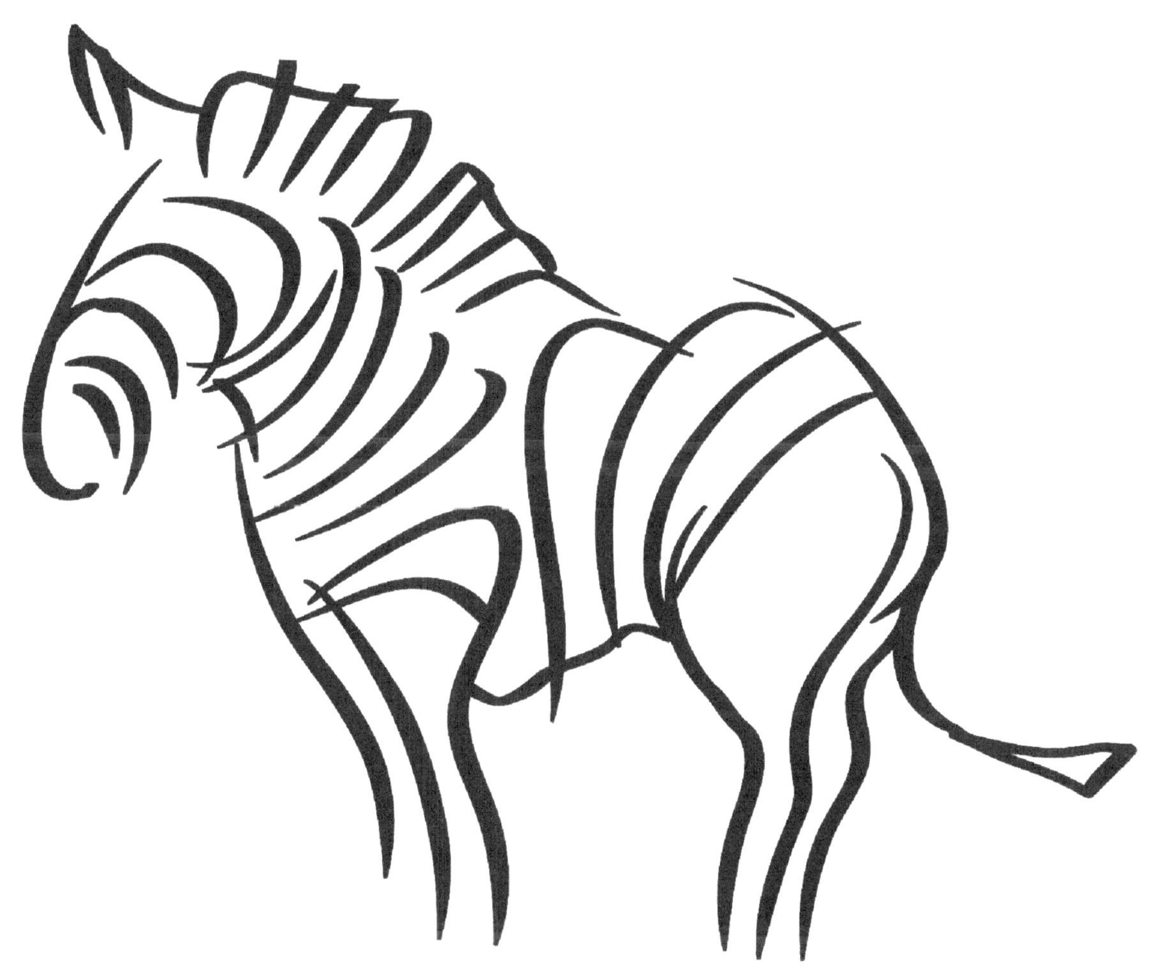